Polly Bemis

Polly Bemis (right) with Nellie Shupp, sister of Charles Shepp. (Note: Nellie spelled her last name Shupp not like her brother, Shepp.) Photo courtesy of Peter Klinkhamer.

Idaho County's Most Romantic Character:

Polly Bemis

By
Sister M. Alfreda Elsensohn
O.S.B., M.S. (Ed.)

First printing, January 1976
Second printing, December 1987
Third printing, May 2016

IDAHO CORPORATION
OF BENEDICTINE SISTERS
Cottonwood, Idaho

Copyright 1979 by Sister Alfreda Elsensohn
Cottonwood, Idaho

All rights reserved.

Published in the United States by
Twin Towers Publishing
Info: twintowers@stgertrudes.org

ISBN 978-0-9858830-2-7

Table of Contents

Chapter		Page
I.	Charles Bemis Arrives at Warren	9
II.	Polly's Early History	14
III.	Polly Nurses a Wounded Man	19
IV.	Polly and Charles are Married	22
V.	Neighbors Across the River	28
VI.	Fire and Death Strike Polly	35
VII.	Polly's Illness and Death	40
	Epilogue	44

References:
Bailey, R. G, *River of No Return,* 1935
Peterson, Harold, *The Last of the Mountain Men,* 1969
National Geographic, July 1936
The Pony Express, February 1970, Sonora, California
Adkinson, Loyal; typed interview with Taylor Smith
Bancroft, George J.; typescript of Polly Bemis story
Newell, Helen M.; typed paper on Polly Bemis
Letters from H. J. Swinney, J. F. Safley, Peter Klink-
 Hammer, Taylor Smith, Effie Miller, and others
Newspaper articles from *Spokesman Review, Lewiston Tribune,* and *Idaho County Free Press*

List of Illustrations

		Page
Frontispiece:	Nellie Shupp, sister of Charles Shepp with Polly to the right	2
Plate I.	Charles A. Bemis, early picture taken in Connecticut	10
Plate II.	Bemis Gold Scales	11
Plate III.	Gold trinket made by Polly for Caroline Bancroft	16
Plate IV.	Polly's crochet work	17
Plate V.	Jewelry brought from China by Polly, given to Mrs. Ada Cyr in 1896 in Florence	17
Plate VI.	Polly's Wedding Dress	23
Plate VII.	Warren Hotel ---The white house nearby belonged to Bemis. Here Bemis and Polly were married. Taylor Smith was at the wedding	24
Plate VIII.	Certificate of Residence	25
Plate IX.	Bemis Boat Landing, Bemis operated a ferry but never charged anything for crossing travelers	26
Plate X.	Polly and Bemis with horse at their Salmon River home. Notice the steep terrain in the background	27
Plate XI.	Two prospectors located across the river at the mouth of Crooked Creek	28

List of Illustrations

		Page
Plate XII.	Sister Theresa and Sister Alfreda at Orogrande Summit, near the mailman's cabin in the boom days of Buffalo Hump	29
Plate XIII.	Buffalo Hump and Buffalo Lake, old miner's cabin on hillside	29
Plate XIV.	Jacob Shepp, Charlie's father, feeding deer in the Shepp-Klinkhammer orchard	30
Plate XV.	There is a cabin here.	31
Plate XVI.	Looking toward War Eagle Camp	31
Plate XVII.	Captain Guleke on the Salmon	32
Plate XVIII.	Polly in center, the lady with the hat was Mrs. Patterson of newspaper fame and one of the other women was a Norwegian princess	33
Plate XIX.	Shepp and Klinkhammer's boat crossing, especially handy at the time of the first Bemis house burned to the ground	35
Plate XX.	Polly and her dog. Teddy died in the fire of first cabin	36
Plate XXI.	Polly's chickens	36
Plate XXII.	Polly and Charles Bemis at home	37
Plate XXIII.	Peter Klinkhammer in front of Polly's cabin	40
Plate XXIV.	Peter Klinkhammer donating the last of Polly's souvenirs to St. Gertrude's Museum in 1964	41
Plate XXV.	Territorial Idaho Centennial	45
Plate XXVI.	Charles Bemis with his dog	46
Plate XXVII.	Polly looking toward her garden	47

CHAPTER ONE

Charles Bemis Arrives at Warren

RICH PLACER FIELDS of Central Idaho were discovered just after the Civil War. It was a "poor man's camp." The pay streaks were small but rich, and there was an abundance of water and timber. To offset the natural advantages, the locality was very inaccessible. Distance was not the only obstacle. Central Idaho is an extremely rough and mountainous country and the yearly snowfall often was twelve feet deep at Warren where the story begins.

Warren was a typical mining camp of the day. There was one crooked street parallel to the gold-bearing gulch and each side was lined with saloons, dance halls, bunk houses, hotels and stores. All buildings were built of logs, even the floors were hewn logs.

Charles Bemis was rather an unusual man to come to Warren. He came with his father, a Connecticut jeweler, and was of the old Bemis family. C. A. Helping was his father's partner in the mines. Charlie was well educated, tall, rather frail and rather averse to hard work. He had neither the physical strength nor the natural aptitude to build sluices or dig gold gravel. He went to work in the mines, however, and he acquired some good claims.

His natural instinct brought him back to the comparative comforts of Warren when it was possible. He was fond of playing cards and gradually became the town's best poker player. He found he could win more money playing poker than he could make as a miner and besides, he liked it better, so he sold or leased his mining claims.

One of his earliest chores when he first arrived was to help with the dance hall. The mining community at Warren, then known as Washington, was thirsty for entertainment.

*Charles A. Bemis, early picture taken in Connecticut.
Photo courtesy of Peter Klinkhamer.*
PLATE I

Bemis' gold scales.
Photo courtesy of the Historical Museum at St. Gertrude.
PLATE II

Bemis was a violinist, but had no instruments or musicians and no music for dances. Bemis would get people to whistle or sing selections and man named Peter Bemer would write the notes in shorthand on paper ruled like music paper.

By 1958, I had heard of his famous book of music and stopped at New Meadows to interview the owner of the precious book. Mr. Taylor Smith knew Charlie Bemis very well though he did not receive the book directly from him, but from a man named Charlie Brown.

The cover of the book was made of canvas, 13 inches by 8 inches. The words "C. A. Bemis" were sketched plainly on the outside with the C partially defaced. On the front page, with pencil, he had written "C. A. Bemis. Date 1864, Camp Washington, Warren's diggings." There were 75 pages in the book.

During the interview I jotted down the names of a few selections: Waltz from Uncle John, St. Patrick's Day in the Morning, Schottische from Henry Redberg, Waltz by John of Amador County, California, Polka Mazurka.

Realizing the historic value of the book, I wrote to

Mr. H. J. Swinney, then director of music of the Idaho State Historical Society. Soon after he received my letter, Mr. Swinney managed to visit with Taylor Smith at New Meadows and asked to see the book. Mr. Smith did not want to let the book out of his hands for a moment.

He told Mr. Swinney that the book would eventually go to his stepson, Noel Krigbaum of Boise. Mr. Sweeney was able to contact Mr. Krigbaum and borrow the book for reproduction by a Music Society in Boise for the sum of $75. Thus, the State Museum had a copy.

At the time of the Idaho Centennial 1963, there was discussion about the original centennial music of Idaho and what it should be. John Lister, musical director of Sun Valley, began to check at the State Museum and found the manuscript book of the town dances of the mining town of Warren. On the record they were recorded as they would have been played by piano or violin. Several Grangeville ladies of the Idaho County Historical Societhy recognized them after I told them about the origin. Senator Church provided a prologue and Governor Smilie's voice was also heard.

After Bemis had opened his gambling place, he had the attraction of the Hurdy Gurdy girls, like most mining camps. They were dance hall girls generally recruited in Germany, coming and working as a group of from four to six girls. Miners bought a ticket at the saloon bar, paying from fifty cents to a dollar, which they gave to the girl they wanted to dance with.

When a miner thought he could afford a wife and wanted one of these girls, he would pay the balance due the agent and get the girl, providing she was willing. Dancing was the only obligation that these girls had to the miner, the saloon, or the agent. Many of these girls did, however, find husbands and they became mothers of early pioneer families.

Back to Bemis and his poker, like most keen gamblers, Bemis cared little for drink but he prospered as it was and apparently was on his road to riches. His great reputation for square dealing brought him certain responsibilities which were not entirely pleasing. It was and is the habit of miners and cowboys and timber jacks to safeguard their "pile" by giving some of it to a true friend before setting out for a good time. So Bemis procured a big wooden safe in which to keep the gold dust and that of his depositors. For instance, a miner would come from digging with six buckskin bags of gold dust and nuggets. He would go to Bemis and say, "I'm to have a little celebration, Charlie, but don't give this to me until I am absolutely sober again." So Charles Bemis would put the "pile" in his big wooden safe and keep it there until the morning after had really arrived, when he would deliver it back to its grateful owner.

CHAPTER TWO

Polly's Early History

POLLY, ORIGINALLY KNOWN AS Lalu Nathoy, was born in 1853 in the north of China near the Mongolian border where brigands for centuries had been sweeping down to raid the countryside. Her family was very poor, farming a small plot of ground, and when they weren't suffering from the plundering of brigands, their crops were burning up with drought. There came a year of great famine, when there was not only the drought but the outlaws galloped down out of the north and stripped the farmers of what little grain there was, leaving them destitute.

To keep the rest of the family from starvation, Lalu's father traded her to the brigands in exchange for enough seed to plant another crop. She was sold to an outfit that shipped women slaves to the New World. She was 18 when she arrived on the West Coast and probably 19 when she came to Warren.

All Chinese in this country were controlled by an organization known as the Six Companies, a wealthy group in San Francisco. Polly said that an old woman brought her from San Francisco to Portland. It seems that Hong King bought her for $2500, sight unseen. When Polly came into Warren with his pack train, a stranger helped her off the horse and called her Polly. Then someone called into Charlie's open door, "Charlie, this is Polly."

The leader, Hong King, took Polly with him, the girl with the pink cheeks and shy modest ways, to be his cook and slave. Her feet were deformed, indicating that they had been bandaged in early childhood. She wore a size 13 shoe. From this we may assume that for a time at least she had been of a higher class or caste than the peasant class from which these girls were generally recruited.

The Chinese girls made a great hit with the white men but sometimes they were treated roughly. The two Chinese girls who came with Polly were transferred to another camp but Polly was retained as dance hostess.

Next door to Charlie's place of business was the saloon of Hong King. Polly was accustomed in the early afternoon to go to Bemis' room and tidy up the place, which pleased him. Thus he took a personal interest in the little dancing girl.

When things got too rough in Hong King's dance hall, Polly used to fly out the back door into Bemis' back door or, unable to do that, she would call Bemis and he never failed her. His quiet, stern personality together with his shooting ability saved Polly from several very threatening situations.

Charlie Bemis' neighbor was a gambler and proud of his skill at Draw Poker. Charlie Bemis would play any game with anyone. Finally, they met in a game of Draw. The other players were alone. The tide turned and the Chinaman was losing regularly. Sometimes miners had been known to put up their clothes. The stakes were high for either of the champions to give or take clothes.

Polly appeared dressed in yellow. She was the next stake. Bemis shoved the paper transfer and cards. The Chinaman shoved in the paper which transferred Polly. The next morning Polly was moved to one of the twin cabins. The Chinaman was never seen in Warren again. Now that he had won Polly, Bemis asked, "What shall I do with you?"

After that Polly ran a boarding house at Charlie's Place. She was an excellent cook. And she had a marvelous sense of humor. At the boarding house she overheard some men complaining about her coffee. She came running out from behind the stove waving a cleaver and said, "Who no like my coffee?" The late Frank McGrane, Sr., recalled an occasion when a group of young people went to Warren and Polly cooked supper for them.

Polly had been taught the art of goldsmithing and she used to beg nuggets from her friends, especially those who came to her boarding place. She fashioned the nuggets with a hammer and pick and made many trinkets which in turn she sold for a goodly sum.

She made one such trinket for Caroline Bancroft, the daughter of George J. Bancroft, engineer at the War Eagle Mine. Polly reminded C. J. Czizek 30 years later that he had been one of her early boarders. Later he became a State Inspector of Mines.

Another favorite occupation for Polly was crocheting. There are eight pieces of such work in the Museum at St. Gertrude's. She liked to crochet flowers, cats, birds, geese,

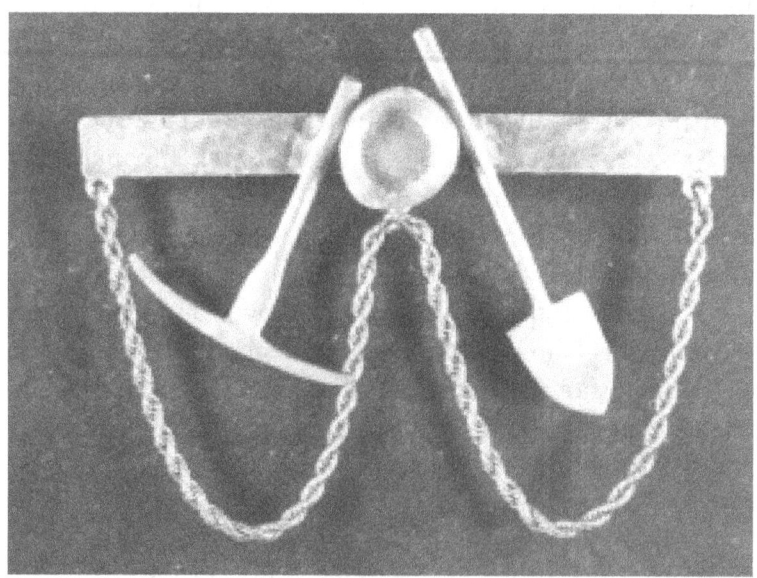

Gold trinket made by Polly for Caroline Bancroft.
PLATE III

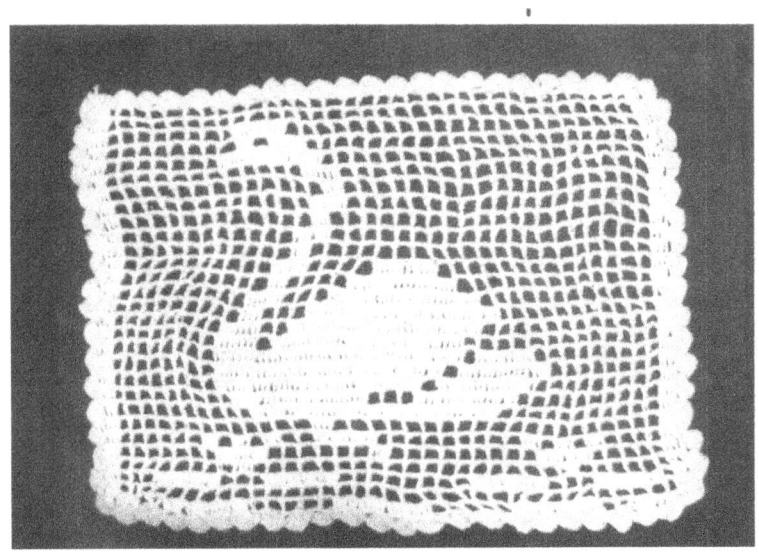

Polly's crochet work.
PLATE IV

Jewelry brought from China by Polly, given to Mrs. Ada Cyr in 1896 in Florence.
PLATE V

and butterflies. She sometimes used red for edging. There are also two pieces of embroidery. These pieces were brought to the museum by Peter Klinkhammer in 1943. He brought the last souvenirs in 1964.

Other items in the museum's collection include Polly's sunbonnet, shawl, a small suitcase, Bemis' gold scales and weights, several large spoons and a set of mother of pearl silverware probably given by friends, six souvenir spoons, a hatpin, Bemis' ring, which Polly made over for Klinkhammer but which he never wore, some lace curtains and three dresses.

A later addition is a brown velvet dress which is 100 years old. Mrs. Ann Copp of Lewiston said that Polly gave this to her when she was five years old. It is lined with black figured cloth. Polly had evidently made it over at one time. Mrs. Copp's mother presented an ivory necklace.

The late Clifford Cyr of Riggins sent three pins, jewelry that Polly had brought with her from China and had given to his first wife, Ada, in 1896, at Florence.

CHAPTER THREE

Polly Nurses a Wounded Man

POLLY HAD BEEN in Warren 18 years when an unusual affair took place. Bemis' place was still open in 1890 and he was still dealing cards to anyone who was interested. He was visiting with his young friend Taylor Smith when Johnny Cox, a half-breed, came along and, leaning against a porch post, said to Bemis, "When I get this cigarette rolled, if you don't give me back that $150 you beat out of me at poker, I'm going to shoot your eye out." Bemis, thinking this was idle talk, continued his conversation with the boy.

But Cox meant everything he said and finished rolling the cigarette. He lit it, then, reaching for his gun, aimed at Bemis' right eye. He missed the eye by less than an inch, the ball slanting back and downward, lodged in the bony part of the skull, back of the left ear.

A door leading to the back room of the saloon was taken off its hinges and used as a litter to carry Bemis to his home about 150 yards away. A call was sent for Dr. Bibby, the 350-pound x-ray surgeon at Grangeville. When Dr. Bibby examined the wound he said: "Nothing can be done. He is too far gone."

The trip to Warren by way of Florence must have been a rugged one for the good doctor, as well as for his team of thoroughbreds and the old beat-up buck-board that he always rode in. Perhaps he was thinking of the road out of Slate Creek when he presented his bill for $500 for services for the well-to-do saloon keeper.

The opinion of the doctor was accepted by the Warren community but not by Polly. Stepping out of her character as a slave, she took command, and went to work to save the life of the man Bemis. A Mr. Troll helped some but Polly went to work with her Chinese herbs and remedies for the man who she had learned to respect and even to love. She removed the bullet from his neck with the help of a razor, cleaned out the festered wound with her crochet hook sterilized no doubt with whiskey, and nursed him back to health. After a month he was able to sit up and smoke but it took much longer for complete recovery.

Immediately after the shooting the people at Warren's Camp raised $300 to pursue Johnny Cox. H. W. Cone traced him to Pocatello and arrested him after nine days. On October 31, 1891, Johnny Cox was sentenced to five years in prison for assault with a deadly weapon. Later the sentence was reduced to two years.

In the beginning, this battle for the life of Bemis won for Polly the respect and admiration of the community in which she lived. In her own right she stood out challenging American womanhood for a place in Western Civilization. Like a butterfly emerging from a cocoon, Polly was now free from the chains of slavery. She had brought warmth and humanness to a time and place that was often bleak and brutal.

The late Taylor Smith said that his parents separated when he was twelve years old and the mother, with her three children, Frankie, Georgie, and Taylor, moved to Warren to run a hotel. There Taylor and Bemis, the saloon keeper, became good friends. Bemis became a counselor to the fatherless boy. Taylor remarked to his cousin, the late Loyal Adkinson, "Charlie and Polly were like father and mother to me, but Charlie would never let me come into the saloon."

Many raised in a more sheltered atmosphere than a rough western mining camp would find it difficult to understand how a teenager could grow up in such surroundings and become anything but a saloon bum. We are surprised when we find that a gambler-saloon operator still mindful of the culture of civilization in which he had been reared, was willing to go out of the way to see that the youth he contacted would not follow in his footsteps.

Virtually all the pioneers brought some reminder of their past with them, perhaps a bit of soil, a plant or a few flower seeds. Most of the young men coming to the camp brought memories of their earlier life, their home, their school, friends and their mother. Charles Bemis it seems was one of those who still wanted to do something good, that he might prove worthy of his past.

To the teenage boy, Bemis became a heroic character and he resolved to follow the seed planted by Bemis, showing that there was a better way to live.

CHAPTER FOUR

Polly and Charles are Married

BY THIS TIME, Bemis not only admired Polly, but loved her. Perhaps Polly also became a beneficiary from the beginning to Charlie Bemis to reappraise and redirect his life, for it was not long before her status was changed to a more respectable position of Mrs. Bemis. They were married August 13, 1894. Polly was now free from the chains of slavery. Taylor Smith witnessed the wedding. Polly highly prized her wedding certificate as wells as her Certificate of Residence for a Chinese Laborer, which she received in 1896.

"This is to certify that on the 13th day of August, 1984, I have joined in the holy bonds of matrimony Chas. A. Bemis and Miss Polly Nathoy at the residence of C. A. Bemis.
August 13th 1894
Warrens, Idaho Co.
Witness
W.J. Kelly   A. D. Smead
George L. Patterson   Justice
                                    of the Peace"

In their later life Charlie and Polly Bemis entertained many people of note in the political and scientific life of the state and nation. The National Geographic Magazine for July 1936 wrote: "For many years the generous hospitality of Polly and her husband was a byword among the mountain people. Her death removed Salmon's most romantic figure."

Polly and Charles are Married 23

Polly's wedding day. Photo courtesy Idaho Historical Society.
PLATE VI

*Warren Hotel -- The white house nearby belonged to Charles Bemis. Here Charles and Polly were married.
Taylor Smith was at the wedding.
Photo courtesy Historical Museum at St. Gertrude.*
PLATE VII

In his "River of No Return," the late R. G. Bailey says: "I visited several times with this couple, and never have I been more courteously entertained. They were hospitality itself, and would take no remuneration for their trouble. She (Polly) has a yellow skin but a white heart encased in a sheathing of gold."

After Polly and Bemis were married, Bemis rented his gambling hall and Polly dug up her caches of "dust" and converted all except about ten pounds of nuggets into five dollar or $2.50 gold pieces. Some of the coins were made into buttons which she could use on her dresses. She would change them from one dress to another at times.

Charlie Bemis' health was not good and he decided to try a more peaceful way of life. He bought some land at the edge of the Salmon River, forty miles upriver from Riggins, reached by a boat. He had a two-story house built on this

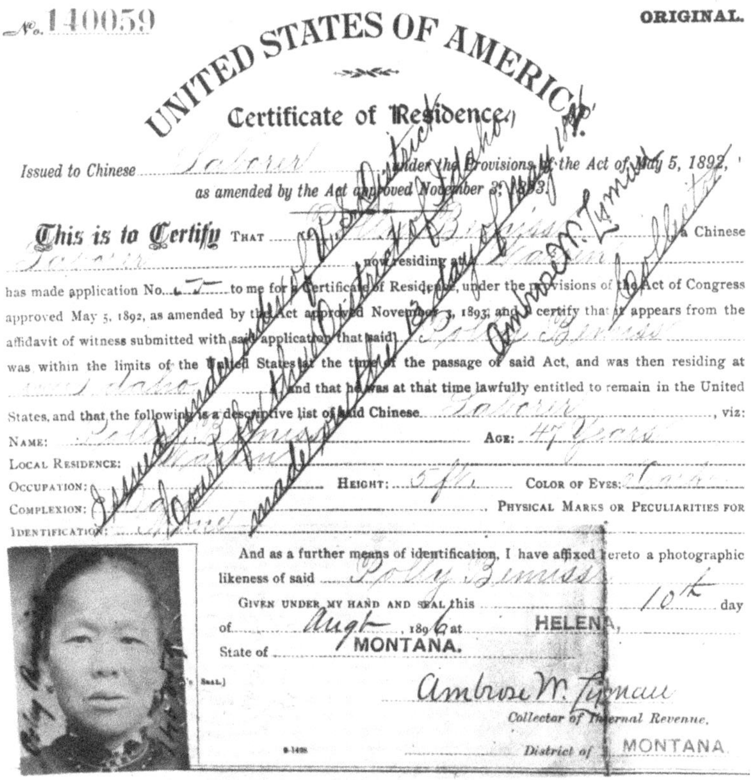
№. 140059 ORIGINAL.

UNITED STATES OF AMERICA.

Certificate of Residence.

Issued to Chinese Laborer, under the Provisions of the Act of May 5, 1892, as amended by the Act approved November 3, 1893.

This is to Certify THAT Polly Bemiss, a Chinese Laborer now residing at Warren, has made application No. 7 to me for a Certificate of Residence, under the provisions of the Act of Congress approved May 5, 1892, as amended by the Act approved November 3, 1893, and I certify that it appears from the affidavit of witness submitted with said application that said Polly Bemiss was within the limits of the United States at the time of the passage of said Act, and was then residing at Warren Idaho and that he was at that time lawfully entitled to remain in the United States, and that the following is a descriptive list of said Chinese Laborer, viz:

NAME: Polly Bemiss AGE: 47 Years

LOCAL RESIDENCE: Warren

OCCUPATION: HEIGHT: 5 ft COLOR OF EYES: Dark

COMPLEXION: PHYSICAL MARKS OR PECULIARITIES FOR IDENTIFICATION:

And as a further means of identification, I have affixed hereto a photographic likeness of said Polly Bemiss.

GIVEN UNDER MY HAND AND SEAL this 10th day of Augt, 1896 at HELENA, State of MONTANA.

[SEAL.]

Collector of Internal Revenue, District of MONTANA.

Certificate of Residence. Photo courtesy Peter Klinkhammer.
PLATE VIII

ranch. At first people called it the "Bemis" place, but before long it became the "Polly" place.

Even before Bemis' ordeal people had felt free to call on Polly for anyone sick in Warren. Several writers including R. G. Bailey pictured her in a nursing garb and called her "The Angel of the Salmon River." She was official nurse for anyone who became ill or was injured, whether they could pay or not.

Bemis operated a ferry but never charged anything for crossing travelers. Prospectors continued to pass up and down the river for many years and Polly furnished them with fresh vegetables and fruits, since hers was the only garden on the river. Often she would ask, "Where is Al Talkington?" She had known him from her first days in Warren.

Polly loved this place on the river. She hiked around with Charlie on his hunting trips because her eyes were sharper than his. The canyon was thousands of feet deep, mostly too steep for farming, but on fifteen acres at the base of the canyon Polly raised cherries, pears, plums, grapes, blackberries, watermelons, vegetables, and clover. Her farm childhood had stayed with her and she had the true green thumb.

When they first came to the ranch Charlie started to teach her but after a while he discontinued his lessons. She could add and play cards and was able to make change for prospectors who came to buy food.

Bemis Boat Landing. Bemis operated a ferry but never charged anything for crossing travelers.
Photo courtesy Peter Klinkhammer.
PLATE IX

POLLY AND CHARLES ARE MARRIED   27

*Polly and Bemis with horse at their Salmon River home.
Notice the steep terrain in the background.
Photo courtesy Peter Klinkhammer.*
PLATE X

CHAPTER FIVE

Neighbors Across the River

IN TIME, 1903, two prospectors located across the river at the mouth of Crooked Creek. They were Charlie Shepp and Peter Klinkhammer.

Shepp worked in Seattle for several years and then accompanied Rex Beach to Nome, Alaska. Klinkhammer was one of a family of twelve who came to the Buffalo Hump district when 17 years old. It was there that he met Charlie Shepp and the two became very good friends. During the winter they started work on the house which required a good deal of work to make it liveable. They planned to raise

Two prospectors located across the river at the mouth of Crooked Creek. Photo courtesy Peter Klinkhammer.
PLATE XI

Sister Theresa and Sister Alfreda at Orogrande Summit, near the mailman's cabin in the boom days of Buffalo Hump. Photo courtesy Charles Poxleitner.
PLATE XII

Buffalo Hump and Buffalo Lake, old miner's cabin on hillside. Photo courtesy Phil Shira.
PLATE XIII

produce and sell it to the miners in the Hump and Jumbo. Peter was the carpenter and Shepp was the gardener. Once a year Peter made the six-day round trip to Grangeville via Concord and Adams Camp to get the years' necessities. They were soon in business at $500 each.

In 1961 Klinkhammer commented to a Free Press reporter: "It takes 10 minutes to fly. It used to take two or three days to walk out." His post offices changed communities. The successsion of posts included Hump, Concord, Callender, Jumbo, Orogrande, Dixie, and McCall. He always took his citizenship seriously even if he had to ride 20 miles on horseback to vote.

Charlie Shepp and Peter Klinkhammer became the most loyal friends the Bemis couple had, watching over them for the rest of their lives. Charlie Bemis' health was not good and kept going downhill so that by 1919 he was an invalid. It was said that he had tuberculosis.

Jacob Shepp, Charlie's father, feeding deer in the Shepp-Klinkhammer orchard.
Photo courtesy Peter Klinkhammer.
PLATE XIV

There is a cabin here.
Photo courtesy Peter Klinkhammer.
PLATE XV

Looking toward War Eagle Camp.
Photo courtesy Caroline Bancroft.
PLATE XVI

The two prospector friends strung a telephone line the one-half mile from their ranch across the river to the Polly place and checked on them regularly. Polly loved the telephone. "How many eggs you get today? Six? I got ten," and she would go off into gales of giggles. "How many fish you catch? None? You no good. You fella come over Sunday. I cook great big fish I catch today."

Now and then, riverman Captain Harry Guleke stopped at the Polly place while on a tour down the river. In July 1921, he stopped to allow the Countess Gizycka, Eleanor Medill Patterson, to meet Polly. "Polly told me – for we took to each other at once - part of her story, soto voce, darting her wise old eyes about to see if the others were listening. 'My folluks in Hong Kong had no grub. De sellee me… slave girl. Old woman smuggle me into Portland. I cost $2500. Don't look it now, hmmm!' she chuckled. 'Old Chinee man he took me along to Warren's in a pack train. I never seen a railroad.'"

Captain Guleke on the Salmon River.
Photo courtesy Peter Klinkhammer.
PLATE XVII

Down the River of No Return with Captain Guleke. Polly in the center, the lady with the hat was Mrs. Patterson of newspaper fame and one of the other women was a Norwegian princess. Photo courtesy Peter Klinkhammer.
PLATE XVIII

Mrs. Patterson spoke for Polly's quality and indicated that she was enchanted with her. "Five feet tall, she is brown and wrinkled as a nut," she wrote, "and at 69, full of dash and charm."

At the turn of the century Captain Guleke charged $1000 for a trip down the River of No Return. He made his first trip for a mining engineer in 1902 to Lewiston. He once went as far as Portland. Later on in life he married a widow. He never had any children but made it a point to carry oranges and candy which he would toss to children on the river bank.

In 1930, Guleke was nearly 70 years old and floated the river less frequently. He died at his home in Salmon and is buried in the town cemetery. His grave stone carries the simple and appropriate inscription "The River of No Return."

CHAPTER SIX

Fire and Death Strike Polly

IN 1922, THE BEMIS house caught fire and burned to the ground. Polly and Shepp got Charlie safely out but little else was saved. Two months later Charlie died and was buried on the Shepp property. Klinkhammer arrived after the fire and was able to save Polly's chickens but they lost Teddy, Polly's dog.

*Shepp and Klinkhammer's boat crossing, especially handy at the time the first Bemis house burned to the ground.
Photo courtesy Peter Klinkhammer.*
PLATE XIX

Polly and her dog, Teddy, who died in the fire of the first cabin. Photo courtesy Peter Klinkhammer
PLATE XX

Polly with her chickens. Photo courtesy Peter Klinkhammer
PLATE XXI

FIRE AND DEATH STRIKE POLLY

*Polly and Charles Bemis at home.
Photo courtesy Idaho Historical Society.*
PLATE XXII

Klinkhammer took Polly by horseback to Warren for the winter. While she was still grieving over the loss of her husband, he took her to Boise to see the Idanha Hotel, her second movie show, her first high building and an elevator, all in one day.

"My husband say we will never see railroad and then he die, then I go to dentist. Now I see Boise, big city stores, streetcars run into middle of the street. Lots of people. I like it but it makes me tired to look so much."

While in Grangeville, Polly visited Mrs. Bertha Long, whom she had met long years ago in Warren. When Mrs. Long's parrot suddenly began to chatter, "What does Polly want for breakfast?" the Chinese woman was puzzled and wanted to know how the bird knew her name. Mrs. Long explained that the bird's name was Polly too.

The parrot was a large green bird with gold and green wings and Polly called it a talkee bird. She said, "This is the first talkee bird me see um since I leave um Shanghai. Most birds in Shanghai talkee hi-yu bad; this talkee bird talkee nice."

Ralph D. Long told another story. Bemis once captured a cougar and kept it as a pet for some time, evidently, in the Salmon River home. The cat ate with them from a tin plate nailed to the table. Polly remarked, "Charlie kept um big cat but wen stranger come he hump um put and spit un." Eventually the cougar had to be put away.

When school came to Warren, Polly remarked, "I can't go to school, I got to make money. God gave me that much," she said pointing to her head. "I learn right along." It was probably at this time that John Carrey's sister lived with Polly in Warren while she went to school. Polly gave her the original photo taken in Warren at her wedding which I believe she still has.

In the spring, Polly's good neighbors, Shepp and Klinkhammer, built a new log house on her ranch with bed, chairs, and table. She was now nearly seventy years old and she made an agreement with them that if they would watch out for her, she would deed her personal property to them. They took care of her heavy gardening and provided her with food and game. And since she couldn't read or write, Shepp's diary constantly noted, "Ordered garden seeds for Polly," and "Measured Polly for dress and ordered from Montgomery Ward."

In 1923 friends took Polly on a trip to Grangeville. She had her first ride in an automobile, she saw a train and her first movie and she came home with a new dress, hat and white shoes, and a grip full of new clothes.

When Polly left Grangeville she said, "Maybe I come back next year; it take hiyu money but maybe I come back?"

It was during this Grangeville visit that the late J. F. Safley, editor of the Idaho County Free Press from 1923-24, wrote picturesquely to the author after he had read Volume I, "Pioneer Days in Idaho County."

He said, "I interviewed Polly Bemis in 1923, when she, like a modern Rip Van Winkle, emerged from half a century's slumber beneath the shadow of majestic Buffalo Hump." He added, "Your book appears to be accurate whereas most histories are not." He expressed pleasure at the way I had used newspaper clippings. In 1953, Mr. Safley was killed in a plane accident in Mexico.

CHAPTER SEVEN

Polly's Illness and Death

POLLY'S SECOND CABIN still stands in the flat by the creek that bears her name. The name was suggested by Shepp and Klinkhammer to the government survey party that floated down the river in 1911. They thought that Polly might be remembered longer than Bemis.

The two friends Shepp and Klinkhammer continued to look after her until she became ill in 1933. Then the two men took her on horseback to the War Eagle Mine and there an ambulance sent by the county sheriff was waiting for her with a nurse. It took nine hours to get to Grangeville where she was placed in a nursing home.

Peter Klinkhammer in front of Polly's cabin.
Photo courtesy Idaho Historical Society.
PLATE XXIII

Polly's Illness and Death

In 1942, the late Mr. Frank McGrane, Sr., recalled a visit with Polly when she was ill in Grangeville. Polly said to him, "Charlie wouldn't have died so soon but he just sat around till he was of no account."

Mrs. Bertha Long also visited her and she said, "You'll soon get well." But Polly answered, "No, me too old to get well, me have to go to other world to get well."

Polly died on November 6, 1933. She had expressed a wish to be buried down by the roaring Salmon but since neither Shepp nor Klinkhammer could be located at the time of her death, she was buried in Prairie View Cemetery at Grangeville when the Depression made county funds for the burial rather low. Shepp died in 1936 and was laid to rest on the Salmon beside Bemis.

Peter Klinkhammer donating the last of Polly's souvenirs to the Historical Museum at St. Gertrude.
Photo courtesy Ladd Arnoti.
PLATE XXIV

Peter Klinkhammer contributed much to the writing of "Pioneer Days in Idaho County." He would send me a check and the orders for copies for numerous relatives and once he added, "We'll put Idaho on the map." He seemed proud of the part he had played in furnishing information for the books.

Mr. Klinkhammer had been visiting a niece in Wenatchee when he became ill, was hospitalized and died on May 2, 1970, at the age of 89. In accordance with his sister's wish, he was buried in Grangeville, Idaho. Three Benedictine sisters attended the Rosary in the funeral chapel the evening before the funeral. Four sisters were again present the next morning at the Mass in Sts. Peter and Paul Catholic Church and at the cemetery rites. In the afternoon, relatives came to St .Gertrude's Museum to view the items of the Polly Bemis collection.

During his lifetime, Mr. Klinkhammer had always intended to buy a tombstone for Polly's grave. The heirs to his estate purchased a stone and thus carried out his desire to have a permanent marker on her grave. The marker reads:

Polly Bemis
Sept. 11, 1853-Nov. 6, 1933

Rather recently Mrs. Earl McDonald told me that she takes care of Klinkhammer's and Polly's graves. The former visited the McDonalds at various times as he was related to them. Mr. McDonald would bring him up to St. Gertrude's Museum to see the author and the Museum.

The late Mrs. Nellie Shultz, widow of a Buffalo Hump miner, often visited Polly in her home on the banks of the Salmon across from the mouth of Crooked Creek. She never tired of proclaiming the nobility and character of Polly Bemis. Because of this lady's respect and esteem for Polly, her other friends have attempted to stress the nobility of character that dominated the mind and purpose in the life of this Chinese woman who stands out today as Idaho County's most romantic character.

A piece of wrapping paper found among Polly's souvenirs reads in the upper corner, "from Mrs. A. P. Schulz, 526 W South Street 1st St. Grangeville, Idaho" and it is addressed to Mrs. Polly Bemis, Dixie, Idaho." No date is given.

EPILOGUE

IN 1935 PETER KLINKHAMMER began to deal with the Filers at Orogrande and Elk City. The war beckoned them and my brother welcomed his former high school student when Paul Filer, a mailman, delivered mail in the vicinity of the Philippines to the ship on which this brother was serving.

When the war was over, the Filers returned to Elk City but Paul had previously visited the Shepp Ranch and dreamed of living there. Klinkhammer would not sell the ranch but finally they agreed to a cooperative cattle raising agreement. Peter retained the right to live on the ranch. Peter Klinkhammer thus lived with the Filers, especially in the summers, and so added immeasurably to the length of his days.

The Filers no longer live on the Shepp ranch but Jim Campbell, an ex-nuclear physicist from the Atomic Energy Project at Idaho Falls, and his wife live there with facilities for 20 guests. Shepp Guest Ranch is disturbed only by the voice of the Salmon River and the cry of the wind. Warren, population 5, lies 15 miles to the south. Dixie, population 18, lies to the north, and Riggins, 40 miles downstream, has about 600 people.

Charles Bemis with his dog.
PLATE XXVI

Polly looking toward her garden.
PLATE XXVII

Other books by Sister Alfreda Elsensohn:

Pioneer Days in Idaho County, Vol. I
Pioneer Days in Idaho County, Vol. II
Idaho Chinese Lore
A Flora of the Camas Prairie Region in the Vicinity of Cottonwood, Idaho

www.ingramcontent.com/pod-product-compliance
Lightning Source LLC
Chambersburg PA
CBHW052031290426
44112CB00014B/2462